Friday Night Takeaway

igloobooks

Published in 2015
by Igloo Books Ltd
Cottage Farm
Sywell
NN6 0BJ
www.igloobooks.com

Image credits: Front cover: tl, cl, bl © StockFood UK, bc, br © PhotoCuisine UK
Back cover: tr, cl © PhotoCuisine UK
All additional images © Thinkstock / Getty

Endpapers: Front: tl, tr, bl, br; Back: tl, tr, bl, br © PhotoCuisine UK
All additional images © Thinkstock / Getty

HUN001 0515
2 4 6 8 10 9 7 5 3 1
ISBN 978-1-78440-232-7

Printed and manufactured in China

Contents

Introduction

Friday night is the perfect night to branch out and try something different for dinner. Celebrate the end of the week by cooking delicious food with family and friends.

Not everyone has hours and hours to spend creating exotic meals, but that doesn't mean that you can't have variety and excitement in your diet. You don't need to travel the world to discover fresh, inspiring food – make it yourself from the comfort of your own kitchen!

This book takes classic dishes from countries around the world and shows you how to recreate them at home – perfect for Friday night feasts! Discover mouth-watering, easy-to-follow recipes, from fragrant Japanese and Thai meals and the spices of the Middle East to authentic European dishes and North American classics. There are even a few tempting sweet treats included for you to try.

Each recipe has been specially written with the home cook in mind. They're straightforward to prepare and you don't need to spend hours cooking them.

Each chapter focuses on a different continent, so that you can easily find the food that defines the region it's from. From tagine to tacos, pizza to pulled pork, there's something to tempt every palate.

So next time you fancy cooking something simple and different on Friday night, try a recipe from this book and bring the tastes and aromas of another continent to your kitchen.

Salmon and vegetable shawarma

Catching up

AFRICA & THE MIDDLE EAST

Cooking together

Malva pudding

Chicken and Peanut Soup

Serves: 4   Preparation time: 15 minutes   Cooking time: 25 minutes

INGREDIENTS

2 tbsp sunflower oil
1 onion, finely chopped
2 cloves of garlic, minced
salt and freshly ground black pepper
1 tsp paprika
2 large skinless chicken breasts, sliced
750 ml / 1 pint 6 fl. oz / 3 cups chicken stock
400 ml / 14 fl. oz / 1 ¾ cups coconut milk
2 tbsp peanut butter
150 g / 5 oz / 1 cup okra, sliced
75 g / 3 oz / ¾ cup peanuts, roughly chopped
2 tbsp coconut flakes
a few sprigs of coriander (cilantro),
    to garnish

METHOD

- Heat the oil in a large saucepan set over a medium heat, then add the onion, garlic and a little salt and sweat for 4–5 minutes.

- Add the paprika and stir well, then add the chicken. Continue to cook for 1 minute, then cover with the stock and coconut milk.

- Bring to a simmer and cook steadily for 10 minutes, then stir through the peanut butter and okra.

- Continue to cook for 8–10 minutes until the okra is tender and the chicken is cooked through.

- Adjust the seasoning to taste, then ladle the soup into bowls. Garnish with chopped peanuts, coconut flakes and sprigs of coriander before serving.

Tabbouleh

Serves: 4   Preparation time: 20 minutes

INGREDIENTS

175 g / 6 oz / 1 cup couscous
3 tbsp extra-virgin olive oil
1 medium cucumber, peeled and diced
150 g / 5 oz / 1 cup cherry tomatoes,
    finely chopped
1 shallot, finely chopped
a small bunch of mint, finely chopped
salt and freshly ground black pepper

METHOD

- Place the couscous in a large, heatproof bowl and pour over boiling water to cover by 1 cm (½ in).
- Cover the bowl tightly with cling film and set to one side for 15 minutes until the couscous has absorbed all of the water.
- Fluff the couscous with a fork, then stir through the olive oil, cucumber, tomatoes, shallot and mint.
- Season to taste, then spoon into a bowl and serve.

Salmon and Vegetable Shawarma

Serves: 4   Preparation time: 10–15 minutes   Cooking time: 10 minutes

INGREDIENTS

2 tbsp olive oil
1 clove of garlic, minced
450 g / 1 lb / 3 cups skinless salmon fillet,
    cubed
salt and freshly ground black pepper
400 g / 14 oz / 5 cups mixed wild
    mushrooms, brushed clean
a small handful of basil leaves,
    roughly chopped
4 medium flour tortillas

METHOD

- Heat the olive oil in a large sauté pan set over a moderate heat until hot.
- Add the garlic and fry for 30 seconds, stirring frequently, then add the salmon and some seasoning.
- Fry for 2–3 minutes, stirring occasionally, then add the mushrooms and continue to fry for 4–5 minutes until tender and starting to brown.
- Stir through the basil and adjust the seasoning to taste, then remove the pan from the heat.
- Heat a large, dry frying pan over a moderate heat until hot. Sprinkle the tortillas with a little water and toast in the pan for 30–45 seconds, turning once, until aromatic and starting to brown.
- Fill the tortillas with the salmon and vegetable filling, then wrap and serve.

Chicken with Giant Couscous

Serves: 4   Preparation time: 15 minutes   Cooking time: 50 minutes

INGREDIENTS

3 tbsp olive oil
salt and freshly ground black pepper
8 small skinless chicken thighs
1 small onion, finely chopped
2 cloves of garlic, minced
1 tsp ras el hanout
400 g / 14 oz / 2 cups canned chopped
    tomatoes
1 l / 1 pint 16 fl. oz / 4 cups chicken stock
1 large red pepper, diced
250 g / 9 oz / 1 ½ cups giant couscous
200 g / 7 oz / 1 cup canned chickpeas
    (garbanzo beans), drained
a large handful of rocket (arugula),
    to garnish

METHOD

- Heat 2 tbsp of oil in a casserole dish set over a
  moderate heat until hot.
- Season the chicken generously and brown in batches,
  then remove to a plate.
- Reduce the heat a little, then add the onion, garlic and
  a little salt. Sauté for 3–4 minutes, then stir in the ras
  el hanout and chopped tomatoes.
- Cook for a further minute, then add a quarter of the
  stock and return the chicken thighs and any juice to
  the pan. Stir well.
- Cover with a lid and cook over a slightly reduced heat
  for 30–40 minutes until the chicken is cooked through.
- Heat the remaining oil in a saucepan set over a
  medium heat, then add the red pepper and sauté for
  3 minutes until softened.
- Add the couscous and chickpeas and cook for
  1 minute, then cover with the remaining stock.
- Bring to a simmer and cook steadily for 8–10 minutes
  until tender. Drain if necessary and season to taste.
- Once the chicken is cooked through, season it to taste,
  then spoon onto plates and serve with the couscous
  and rocket.

Speedy Lamb Tagine

Serves: 4   Preparation time: 20 minutes   Cooking time: 40–45 minutes

INGREDIENTS

4 tbsp olive oil
salt and freshly ground black pepper
750 g / 1 lb 10 oz / 5 cups boneless lamb
     shoulder, trimmed and diced
½ turnip, peeled and finely diced
2 large carrots, peeled and sliced
1 large courgette (zucchini), diced
1 green pepper, finely diced
1 red pepper, finely diced
1 tbsp harissa
½ tsp ras el hanout spice mix
750 ml / 1 pint 6 fl. oz / 3 cups lamb stock
½ preserved lemon, sliced
a few sprigs of flat-leaf parsley, to garnish

METHOD

- Set a tagine or casserole dish over a medium-high heat and add 2 tbsp of olive oil.

- Season the lamb and seal in batches until golden, then remove to a plate.

- Reduce the heat slightly and pour away all but 1 tbsp of the drippings, then add the remaining olive oil.

- Add the turnip and carrots with a little salt and sweat for 6–7 minutes until softened, then add the courgette and peppers.

- Continue to cook for 2 minutes, then stir in the harissa and the ras el hanout.

- Cook for 1 minute, then return the lamb and cover with the stock. Stir well and bring to a simmer.

- Cover and cook over a slightly reduced heat for 40–45 minutes until the lamb is tender, then season to taste and ladle into bowls.

- Serve with a garnish of preserved lemon and parsley.

Peri-peri Chicken

Serves: 4   Preparation time: 20 minutes   Cooking time: 1 hour 20–30 minutes

INGREDIENTS

3 red chillies (chilies), deseeded
1 lemon, juiced
1 tbsp smoked paprika
1 tsp dried oregano
4 cloves of garlic
3 tbsp distilled vinegar
2 tbsp olive oil
salt and freshly ground black pepper
1 x 1.5 kg / 3 lb 5 oz chicken, cleaned with
    wishbone removed
assorted chilli (chili) peppers, to garnish
a few sprigs of coriander (cilantro)

METHOD

- Preheat the oven to 180°C (160°C fan) / 350F / gas 4.

- Blitz together the chillies, lemon juice, paprika, oregano, garlic, vinegar, oil and seasoning in a food processor.

- Smear the paste onto and inside the chicken, then season again with salt and pepper.

- Place the chicken on a grilling tray or in a roasting tin. Roast for 1 hour 20–30 minutes until the thickest part of the thigh reads at least 74°C / 165F.

- Remove the chicken from the oven and leave to rest, covered loosely with aluminium foil, for 10 minutes.

- Using a sharp knife, cut the chicken into pieces, then serve with a garnish of chilli peppers and coriander.

Grilled Sardines with Harissa

Serves: 4   Preparation time: 10 minutes   Cooking time: 4–5 minutes

INGREDIENTS

4 fresh sardines, gutted and cleaned
salt and freshly ground black pepper
2 tbsp harissa
3 tbsp olive oil
a large handful of mint sprigs

METHOD

- Preheat the grill to a high heat.
- Season the insides of the sardines with salt and pepper, then arrange on a grilling tray.
- Make a few slashes in the skin of each sardine and rub with the harissa.
- Drizzle with olive oil and season the skin with a little salt and freshly ground black pepper.
- Grill for 4–5 minutes, turning once, until the skin is crisp and the flesh is opaque.
- Serve immediately with a garnish of mint.

Falafel and Pitta Bread

Serves: 4   Preparation time: 15 minutes   Cooking time: 22–25 minutes

INGREDIENTS

600 g / 1 lb 5 oz / 3 cups canned cooked
    chickpeas (garbanzo beans), drained
1 shallot, finely chopped
2 cloves of garlic, minced
1 tbsp plain (all-purpose) flour
1 tsp ground cumin
½ tsp paprika
½ tsp baking powder
salt and freshly ground black pepper
55 ml / 2 fl. oz / ¼ cup olive oil, plus extra
    for rolling
125 g / 4 ½ oz / 1 cup golden breadcrumbs
4 white pitta breads, split in half
½ cucumber, finely sliced
1 large carrot, peeled and cut into strips
¼ small red cabbage, shredded

METHOD

- Preheat the oven to 190°C (170°C fan) / 375F / gas 5.
- Mash together the chickpeas, shallot, garlic, flour, ground spices, baking powder and seasoning.
- Take tablespoons of the mixture and shape into round balls between oiled palms, then roll in the breadcrumbs to coat.
- Arrange on a large baking tray and drizzle with olive oil. Bake for 22–25 minutes until golden brown on the outside.
- Remove from the oven and let the falafel cool for a few minutes.
- Fill the pitta breads with vegetables and the falafel before serving.

Grilled Pineapple

Serves: 4   Preparation time: 10 minutes   Cooking time: 4 minutes

INGREDIENTS

1 large ripe pineapple, peeled
3 tbsp caster (superfine) sugar
2 tbsp sunflower oil
150 g / 5 oz / ⅔ cup raw honey
400 g / 14 oz / 1 ¾ cups mascarpone
a small handful of mint leaves, to garnish

METHOD

- Preheat a grill or barbecue until moderately hot.
- Slice the pineapple into thick slices using a sharp chef's knife, then pat dry with kitchen paper and sprinkle both sides with caster sugar.
- Oil the grates of the grill or barbecue with a little oil, then grill the pineapple slices for 2 minutes on each side until lightly charred.
- Remove from the grill and stack on a serving platter. Spoon over the honey and serve with the mascarpone on the side and a garnish of mint leaves.

Malva Pudding

Serves: 4   Preparation time: 15 minutes   Cooking time: 25–30 minutes

INGREDIENTS

1 tbsp sunflower oil, for greasing

275 g / 10 oz / 1 ¼ cups caster (superfine) sugar

2 large eggs

2 tbsp apricot jam (jelly)

75 g / 3 oz / ⅓ cup unsalted butter, melted

1 tsp distilled vinegar

75 ml / 3 fl. oz / ⅓ cup whole (full-fat) milk

150 g / 5 oz / 1 cup plain (all-purpose) flour, sifted

1 tsp baking powder

a pinch of salt

250 ml / 9 fl. oz / 1 cup double (heavy) cream, to serve

75 ml / 3 fl. oz / ⅓ cup water

2 tsp vanilla extract

METHOD

- Preheat the oven to 180°C (160°C fan) / 350F / gas 4 and grease 4 heatproof teacups with sunflower oil.

- Beat together 175 g / 6 oz / ¾ cup of sugar with the eggs in a large mixing bowl using an electric mixer.

- Once pale and thick, add the apricot jam and beat again for a further minute.

- Add 1 tbsp of melted butter as well as the vinegar and milk. Beat briefly, then fold through the flour, baking powder and salt until thoroughly combined.

- Divide the batter between the teacups and arrange on a baking tray.

- Bake for 25–30 minutes until risen and golden on top; a toothpick should come out clean from their centres.

- Remove to a wire rack to cool. Combine the remaining sugar and butter with the cream, water and vanilla extract in a saucepan.

- Bring to a simmer and stir, then leave to cool and thicken slightly. Turn out the puddings and serve with the sauce.

Vegetable
samosas

Relaxing with friends

ASIA

A taste of Asia

Pad Thai

Vegetable Samosas

Serves: 4   Preparation time: 20 minutes   Cooking time: 30 minutes

INGREDIENTS

55 ml / 2 fl. oz / ¼ cup sunflower oil
2 onions, finely sliced
2 cloves of garlic, minced
5 cm (2 in) piece of root ginger,
    peeled and minced
2 tsp ground cumin
2 tsp ground coriander
1 tsp mild curry powder
½ tsp garam masala
salt and freshly ground black pepper
450 g / 1 lb / 3 cups floury potatoes,
    peeled and finely diced
100 g / 3 ½ oz / 1 cup frozen peas, thawed
1 l / 1 pint 18 fl. oz / 4 cups vegetable oil,
    for deep-frying
8 samosa wrappers (use spring roll
    wrappers if not available)
a few sprigs of mint, to garnish

METHOD

- Heat the sunflower oil in a large saucepan set over a medium heat.
- Sweat the onion, garlic and ginger for 6–7 minutes, stirring occasionally, then add the ground spices and seasoning. Stir well.
- Add the potato and stir well, then cover with a lid and reduce the heat a little.
- Once the potato is softened, remove the lid and add the peas. Stir well.
- Adjust the seasoning to taste and cool to one side.
- Heat the vegetable oil in a large heavy-based saucepan to 180°C / 350F.
- Wet the rim of the wrappers with water and fold into a triangle, then form a cone around your fingers, sealing one edge, but keeping the case open.
- Fill the wrappers with the vegetable curry and seal well, wetting the rim again if necessary.
- Deep-fry, in batches of four, for 4–5 minutes. Flip the samosas halfway through cooking.
- Drain on kitchen paper as you deep-fry the remaining samosas.
- Serve the samosas warm with a mint sprig garnish.

Ginger and Spring Onion Prawns

Serves: 4   Preparation time: 5–10 minutes   Cooking time: 5 minutes

INGREDIENTS

2 tbsp groundnut oil
1 tbsp sesame oil
5 cm (2 in) piece of root ginger,
    peeled and finely chopped
2 cloves of garlic, minced
600 g / 1 lb 5 oz / 4 cups fresh prawns
    (shrimp) with tails intact, de-veined
    and peeled
salt and freshly ground black pepper
4 spring onions (scallions), roughly chopped
2 tbsp dark soy sauce
a dash of rice wine

METHOD

- Heat the oils in a large wok set over a high heat
  until hot.
- Add the ginger and garlic and stir-fry for 30 seconds,
  then add the prawns and a little seasoning.
- Stir-fry for 2 minutes or until pink and tender.
- Add the spring onions, soy sauce and rice wine.
  Stir well and continue to cook for 2 minutes.
- Adjust the seasoning to taste before serving.

Spring Rolls

Makes: 8   Preparation time: 30–40 minutes   Cooking time: 20–25 minutes

INGREDIENTS

1.25 l / 2 pints 4 fl. oz / 5 cups groundnut oil
3 skinless chicken breasts, cut into
    thin strips
salt and white pepper
1 tbsp Chinese five-spice
1 tbsp oyster sauce
4 large spring onions (scallions),
    sliced thinly lengthways
2 carrots, peeled and julienned
75 g / 3 oz / 3 cups beansprouts
1 tbsp dark soy sauce, plus extra for serving
1 tsp fresh ginger, grated
16 Chinese pancakes, covered with
    a damp cloth
1 egg yolk, beaten

METHOD

- Heat 2 tbsp of the oil in a large wok set over a high heat until hot.

- Stir-fry the chicken with seasoning for 1–2 minutes, then add the five-spice and oyster sauce.

- Continue to cook for a further 2–3 minutes, then remove from the wok.

- In a mixing bowl, combine the spring onions, carrots, beansprouts, soy sauce, ginger and cooked chicken; toss well.

- On a flat surface, lay two of the Chinese pancakes on top of one another.

- Brush all round the edge with the egg yolk.

- Spoon a few tablespoons of the filling onto the lower section of the pancakes and fold the edges inwards to just cover the filling.

- Bring the bottom edge of the pancake over the filling and begin to carefully roll the pancake until you have the shape of a spring roll.

- Repeat the process for the rest of the spring rolls, then cover with a damp cloth to prevent the pancakes from drying out.

- Heat the remaining groundnut oil in a large, heavy-based saucepan to 180°C / 350F.

- Carefully lower 2 spring rolls at a time into the hot oil and deep-fry for 2–3 minutes until golden brown.

- Remove and drain on kitchen paper before serving with soy sauce on the side.

Aloo Jeera

Serves: 4   Preparation time: 10–15 minutes   Cooking time: 30 minutes

INGREDIENTS

1 kg / 2 lb 4 oz / 6 ⅔ cups floury potatoes,
    peeled and diced
3 tbsp sunflower oil
a pinch of cumin seeds
2 cloves of garlic, minced
1 tbsp ground cumin
1 tsp ground coriander
½ tsp garam masala
salt and freshly ground black pepper
a small handful of chives
a large handful of coriander (cilantro),
    finely chopped

METHOD

- Cook the potatoes in a large saucepan of salted, boiling water for 18–22 minutes until tender. Drain and leave to steam dry for a few minutes.

- Heat the sunflower oil in a large sauté pan set over a moderate heat until hot.

- Add the cumin seeds and garlic, then sauté for 30 seconds or until the seeds start to pop.

- Add the ground spices, stir well and cook for 30 seconds, then add the potatoes.

- Reduce the heat and cook, stirring occasionally, for 4–5 minutes until starting to brown.

- Adjust the seasoning to taste and roughly chop most of the chives.

- Spoon the potatoes into bowls and garnish with the chopped chives, coriander and chive stalks on top before serving.

Chicken and Cashew Nut Salad

Serves: 4   Preparation time: 15 minutes   Cooking time: 15–18 minutes

INGREDIENTS

100 ml / 3 ½ fl. oz / ½ cup groundnut oil
2 large chicken breasts
salt and freshly ground black pepper
2 tbsp rice wine
a pinch of caster (superfine) sugar
1 small Chinese cabbage, shredded
150 g / 5 oz / 1 cup sprouting chickpeas
   (garbanzo beans)
100 g / 3 ½ oz / 1 cup lightly toasted
   cashew nuts
a small bunch of coriander (cilantro), torn

METHOD

- Heat 2 tbsp of groundnut oil in a large sauté pan set over a moderate heat.

- Season the chicken breasts with salt and pepper and pan-fry for 15–18 minutes, turning occasionally, until the skin is golden brown and the chicken is cooked through; it should reach at least 74°C / 165F on a meat thermometer.

- Remove the chicken from the pan and leave it to rest to one side.

- Whisk together the remaining oil with the rice wine, caster sugar and seasoning.

- Combine the cabbage, chickpeas and cashew nuts in a large mixing bowl and add the dressing. Toss well to coat thoroughly.

- Shred the chicken breasts into strips.

- Arrange the cabbage, chickpeas and cashew nuts in bowls and top with the chicken and coriander before serving.

Chilli Pork Ribs

Serves: 4   Preparation time: 15 minutes   Cooking time: 1 hour 30–40 minutes

INGREDIENTS

1.2 kg / 2 lb 10 oz rack of pork ribs, trimmed
    and cleaned
100 g / 3 ½ oz / ½ cup hoisin sauce
1 tbsp sesame oil
1 tbsp distilled vinegar
1 tbsp dark soy sauce
1 tbsp runny honey
2 tsp Chinese five-spice
freshly ground black pepper
2 red chillies (chilies), finely sliced
1 tbsp white sesame seeds
a few sprigs of rosemary, chopped

METHOD

- Preheat the oven to 180°C (160°C fan) / 350F / gas 4.
- Place the ribs on a large baking tray lined with kitchen foil.
- Whisk together the hoisin sauce, sesame oil, vinegar, soy sauce, honey, Chinese five-spice and plenty of black pepper.
- Rub the mixture into the ribs, coating both sides as evenly as possible.
- Cook the ribs in the oven for 1 hour 30–40 minutes until the meat is tender and juicy.
- Remove from the oven and leave to rest for 5 minutes before cutting and serving garnished with sliced chilli, sesame seeds and rosemary.

Chicken and Sesame Noodles

Serves: 4   Preparation time: 5–10 minutes   Cooking time: 6–7 minutes

INGREDIENTS

2 tbsp groundnut oil
2 large skinless chicken breasts, sliced
salt and freshly ground black pepper
2 cloves of garlic, minced
2 large carrots, peeled and shredded
200 g / 7 oz / 2 cups mangetout
350 g / 12 oz / 3 cups cooked egg noodles
2 tbsp dark soy sauce
a dash of rice wine vinegar
2 tbsp white sesame seeds

METHOD

- Heat 1 ½ tbsp of the groundnut oil in a large wok set over a high heat until hot.
- Add the chicken and stir-fry with a little salt and pepper until lightly golden all over.
- Remove from the wok, then add the remaining groundnut oil.
- Stir-fry the garlic and carrots for 1 minute, then add the mangetout and continue to stir-fry for a further minute.
- Add the noodles and chicken back to the pan along with the soy sauce and a dash of the vinegar.
- Cook for a further 2–3 minutes, tossing with tongs, until the noodles are piping hot throughout.
- Lift into bowls and garnish with sesame seeds before serving.

Satay Chicken

Serves: 4   Preparation time: 15 minutes   Cooking time: 40 minutes

INGREDIENTS

2 tbsp sunflower oil
salt and freshly ground black pepper
4 chicken legs, trimmed
2 Thai red chillies (chilies), deseeded and
    roughly chopped
2 cloves of garlic
1 stalk of lemon grass, smashed
150 g / 5 oz / ⅔ cup smooth peanut butter
250 ml / 9 fl. oz / 1 cup coconut milk
125 ml / 4 fl. oz / ½ cup hot chicken stock
1 tbsp rice wine vinegar
1 tbsp fish sauce
a small bunch of baby spinach leaves,
    washed
55 g / 2 oz / ⅓ cup peanuts, crushed

METHOD

- Heat the sunflower oil in a large casserole dish set over a moderate heat until hot.

- Season the chicken and seal in the hot oil until golden all over, then remove from the dish to a plate.

- Reduce the heat a little and add the chillies, garlic and lemon grass. Sauté for 1 minute, then stir in the peanut butter.

- Let the peanut butter melt and liquefy before whisking in the coconut milk, stock, vinegar and fish sauce.

- Bring to a simmer, then return the chicken legs to the dish.

- Cook at a gentle simmer, covered, for 25–30 minutes until the chicken is cooked through.

- Stir through the spinach leaves until wilted, then season to taste.

- Spoon the satay chicken into bowls and serve with crushed peanuts sprinkled on top.

Stir-fried Udon Noodles

Serves: 4   Preparation time: 10 minutes   Cooking time: 10 minutes

INGREDIENTS

3 tbsp rice wine vinegar

3 tbsp light soy sauce

1 tbsp sesame oil

1 tbsp caster (superfine) sugar

1 lemon, juiced

1 ½ tbsp water

1 tbsp cornflour (cornstarch)

3 tbsp groundnut oil

salt and freshly ground black pepper

250 g / 9 oz rump or flat iron steak,
    sliced thinly

250 g / 9 oz / 1 cup raw prawns (shrimp),
    peeled and de-veined

1 large carrot, peeled and julienned

1 large green pepper, finely sliced

1 Chinese cabbage, shredded

350 g / 12 oz / 3 cups cooked udon noodles

METHOD

- Whisk together the rice wine vinegar, soy sauce, sesame oil, sugar and lemon juice in a small mixing bowl. Add the water and cornflour and whisk again.

- Heat 1 tbsp of the groundnut oil in a large wok set over a moderate heat until hot.

- Season the steak and prawns, then stir-fry for 2 minutes. Remove from the wok.

- Add the remaining oil, followed by the carrot, pepper and cabbage, then stir-fry for 2–3 minutes. Add the noodles.

- Toss well, then add the sauce to the wok along with the beef and prawns. Let the sauce come to the boil, then reduce the heat and leave it to thicken slightly.

- Toss everything a final time before lifting into bowls and serving.

Vegetable Curry

Serves: 4   Preparation time: 10 minutes   Cooking time: 45–50 minutes

INGREDIENTS

3 tbsp sunflower oil
2 large onions, finely chopped
4 cloves of garlic, minced
3 cm (1 in) piece of root ginger,
    peeled and minced
1 tbsp ground coriander
1 tbsp ground cumin
2 tsp ground turmeric
1 tsp garam masala
1 tsp caster (superfine) sugar
250 g / 9 oz / 1 cup plain yoghurt
55 g / 2 oz / ½ cup ground almonds
250 ml / 9 fl. oz / 1 cup water
110 ml / 4 fl. oz / ½ cup double (heavy)
    cream
salt and freshly ground black pepper
1 aubergine (eggplant), diced
1 green pepper, diced
2 large floury potatoes, peeled and cubed
1 tsp mild curry powder
1 Braeburn apple, cored and finely diced
a small bunch of coriander (cilantro),
    leaves picked

METHOD

- Heat the sunflower oil in a large casserole dish set over a moderate heat until hot.
- Add the onions, garlic and ginger and sweat for 7–8 minutes until golden.
- Add the ground spices and sugar, then reduce the heat a little and cook for 1 minute, stirring frequently.
- Continue to cook for a further 2 minutes, then stir through the yoghurt, almonds and water.
- Bring to a simmer, then cook gently for 8–10 minutes, stirring occasionally. Stir in the cream.
- Blitz the sauce in a food processor until smooth, then return to the dish and season to taste.
- Add the aubergine, pepper and potatoes and simmer in the sauce for 20 minutes until tender.
- Ladle the curry into bowls and garnish with a pinch of curry powder, some diced apple and coriander leaves.

Pad Thai

Serves: 4   Preparation time: 10 minutes   Cooking time: 12–15 minutes

INGREDIENTS

3 tbsp fish sauce
3 tbsp rice wine vinegar
2 tbsp cold water
1 lime, juiced
1 tbsp dark soy sauce
1 tbsp dark brown soft sugar
3 tbsp groundnut oil
salt and freshly ground black pepper
2 large skinless chicken breasts, diced
1 shallot, finely chopped
2 cloves of garlic, minced
2 large eggs, beaten
350 g / 12 oz / 3 cups cooked rice noodles
75 g / 3 oz / 2 cups beansprouts
2 tbsp peanuts, crushed
a small bunch of coriander (cilantro),
    finely chopped

METHOD

- Whisk together the fish sauce, vinegar, water, lime juice, soy sauce and sugar in a small mixing bowl until the sugar dissolves.
- Heat 2 tbsp of the oil in a large wok or sauté pan set over a moderate heat until hot.
- Season the chicken, then stir-fry for 4–5 minutes until golden. Remove to a plate and reduce the heat under the wok.
- Add the remaining oil along with the shallot and garlic, then sauté for 2 minutes.
- Return the chicken along with the beaten egg and cook the egg until scrambled, then add the noodles, beansprouts and peanuts and the prepared sauce.
- Toss everything together and cook for 4–5 minutes, tossing frequently, until the noodles are glossy and the sauce has reduced.
- Season to taste, then serve in bowls garnished with coriander.

Thai Red Curry

Serves: 4   Preparation time: 10 minutes   Cooking time: 15–17 minutes

INGREDIENTS

2 tbsp groundnut oil
2 tbsp Thai red curry paste
1 red pepper, finely diced
100 g / 3 ½ oz / ½ cup canned bamboo
  shoots, drained
4 medium skinless chicken breasts, diced
400 ml / 14 fl. oz / 1 ½ cups coconut milk
1 tbsp fish sauce
1 lime, juiced
1 tsp dark brown soft sugar
salt and freshly ground pepper
a small bunch of Thai basil, finely sliced
cooked jasmine rice, to serve

METHOD

- Heat the oil in a large wok or sauté pan set over a moderate heat until hot.
- Add the paste and fry for 1 minute until fragrant and bubbling.
- Add the pepper and bamboo shoots and fry for 1 minute, then add the chicken.
- Stir-fry for 3 minutes, then add the coconut milk and fish sauce.
- Bring to a simmer, then reduce the heat a little and cook for 10–12 minutes until the chicken is cooked through and the sauce is thickened.
- Adjust to taste using lime juice, sugar, salt and pepper.
- Stir through the sliced basil and serve on top of bowls of rice.

Lemon Chicken

Serves: 4   Preparation time: 10 minutes   Cooking time: 10–12 minutes

INGREDIENTS

2 lemons
150 ml / 5 fl. oz / ⅔ cup warm water
2 tbsp honey
2 large chicken breasts, sliced
1 tbsp cornflour (cornstarch)
3 tbsp groundnut oil
2 small onions, sliced
2 cloves of garlic, minced
1 tbsp dark soy sauce
1 tbsp white sesame seeds
300 g / 10 ½ oz / 3 cups cooked rice, to serve

METHOD

- Pare the zest from one of the lemons and finely slice. Juice both lemons into a jug.

- Add the water and honey to the lemon juice and whisk until the honey has dissolved.

- Toss the chicken in the cornflour, shaking off any excess.

- Heat 2 tbsp of the groundnut oil in a large wok set over a high heat until hot.

- Fry the chicken in the oil until it is brown and crisp at the edges, then remove it from the pan and add the remaining oil.

- Stir-fry the onions and garlic for 2–3 minutes, then add the lemon sauce.

- Let the sauce come to a simmer, then reduce the heat a little and cook until thickened.

- Return the chicken to the pan and let it warm through in the sauce for a few minutes. Season with soy sauce and sprinkle over the sesame seeds.

- Serve the lemon chicken on top of cooked rice in bowls; garnish with lemon zest on top.

Egg Custard Tarts

Makes: 12   Preparation time: 30 minutes   Cooking time: 22–25 minutes

INGREDIENTS

225 g / 8 oz / 1 cup unsalted butter, softened
225 g / 8 oz / 1 cup caster (superfine) sugar
300 g / 10 ½ oz / 2 cups plain (all-purpose)
    flour, sifted
10 medium eggs
1 tsp vanilla extract
700 ml / 1 pint 4 fl. oz / 2 ¾ cups water
250 g / 9 oz / 1 cup evaporated milk

METHOD

- Preheat the oven to 200°C (180°C fan) / 400F / gas 6 and line a 12-hole cupcake mould with cupcake cases.

- Combine the butter with half of the sugar and all of the flour and mix well until a dough starts to form.

- Beat one egg with half of the vanilla, then add it to the dough and mix until you have an even, slightly moist dough.

- Divide the dough into 12 balls. Pat down into rounds and use your fingers to press them into the base and sides of the cases.

- Combine the water with the remaining sugar and vanilla extract in a saucepan and cook over a moderate heat until the sugar has dissolved.

- Remove from the heat and leave to cool, then beat the remaining eggs and gently whisk into the water along with the evaporated milk.

- Strain the filling into a jug, then divide between the cases and bake for 22–25 minutes until the pastry is cooked and the filling is set.

- Remove to a wire rack to cool before serving.

Fried Banana

Serves: 4   Preparation time: 10 minutes   Cooking time: 4–6 minutes

INGREDIENTS

1.25 l / 2 pints 4 fl. oz / 5 cups vegetable oil
4 medium bananas, plus extra to serve
100 g / 3 ½ oz / ⅔ cup self-raising flour, sifted
55 g / 2 oz / ⅓ cup cornflour (cornstarch), sifted
2 tbsp caster (superfine) sugar
2 tbsp butter, melted
300 ml / 10 ½ fl. oz / 1 ¼ cups water
1 tbsp icing (confectioners') sugar, to garnish

METHOD

- Heat the oil in a large, heavy-based saucepan to 180°C / 350F.
- Peel the bananas and cut them in half.
- Combine the flour, cornflour and sugar in a large mixing bowl. Whisk in the melted butter and enough water until you have a smooth, pourable batter.
- Using a pair of tongs, dip the banana pieces into the batter to coat evenly, then lift into the hot oil and cook them, in two batches, for 2–3 minutes until crisp and golden.
- Drain on kitchen paper, then serve with extra bananas and a dusting of icing sugar.

Lamb kebabs

Dinner for two

EUROPE

A family night in

Cherry clafoutis

Moules Marinières

Serves: 4   Preparation time: 15 minutes   Cooking time: 6–7 minutes

INGREDIENTS

2 tbsp olive oil
1 large shallot, finely chopped
1 clove of garlic, finely chopped
2 sticks of celery, sliced
salt and freshly ground black pepper
2 plum tomatoes, seeded and diced
600 g / 1 lb 5 oz / 4 cups mussels,
    cleaned with beards removed
175 ml / 6 fl. oz / ¾ cup dry white wine
a small bunch of flat-leaf parsley,
    roughly chopped

METHOD

- Heat the oil in a large saucepan set over a medium
  heat until hot.

- Add the shallot, garlic, celery and a little salt and
  sauté for 3 minutes until softened.

- Add the tomatoes and mussels, then increase the heat
  and stir well.

- Cover with the wine and cover the saucepan with a lid.
  Cook for 3 minutes, shaking the saucepan occasionally,
  until the mussels have opened.

- Discard any mussels that haven't opened and season
  the broth to taste before stirring through the parsley.

- Serve immediately in bowls.

Asparagus Frittata

Serves: 4   Preparation time: 10 minutes   Cooking time: 10–12 minutes

INGREDIENTS

2 tbsp olive oil
350 g / 12 oz / 3 cups asparagus spears,
    woody ends removed
salt and freshly ground black pepper
8 large eggs
75 ml / 3 fl. oz / ⅓ cup whole (full-fat) milk
2 large vine tomatoes, deseeded and sliced
75 g / 3 oz / ¾ cup Cheddar, grated
a few sprigs of rosemary, to garnish

METHOD

- Preheat the oven to 190°C (170°C fan) / 375F / gas 5.

- Heat the olive oil in a large, ovenproof sauté pan set over a medium heat until hot.

- Add the asparagus spears and a little seasoning and sauté for 3 minutes, turning occasionally, until lightly browned.

- Remove the spears from the pan and set to one side. Whisk together the eggs, milk and a little seasoning in a large mixing jug.

- Pour the egg into the pan and leave it to set for 1 minute, then arrange the asparagus and tomato on top. Sprinkle over the cheese and a pinch of seasoning.

- Bake in the oven for 10–12 minutes until the frittata is puffed and golden on top.

- Remove and leave to cool slightly, then turn out and cut into portions.

- Serve with a garnish of rosemary.

Gazpacho

Serves: 4   Preparation time: 10 minutes

INGREDIENTS

3 red peppers, diced
1 tsp caster (superfine) sugar
1 red chilli (chili), deseeded and chopped
2 slices of white bread, crusts removed
    and diced
3 cloves of garlic, minced
400 g / 14 oz / 2 cups passata
400 g / 14 oz / 2 cups canned chopped
    tomatoes
2 tbsp sherry vinegar
75 ml / 3 fl. oz / ⅓ cup extra-virgin olive oil
salt and freshly ground black pepper
2 tbsp sour cream
a few chives, snipped

METHOD

- Blend the peppers in a food processor until finely chopped.
- Add the sugar, chilli, bread, garlic, passata and chopped tomatoes and blend until smooth.
- Add some water to thin the consistency, if desired, then add the vinegar and olive oil.
- Pulse until combined. Season to taste, then pour into bowls.
- Serve with a swirl of sour cream and some chives.

Bruschetta

Serves: 4   Preparation time: 10 minutes   Cooking time: 5 minutes

INGREDIENTS

8 thick slices of sourdough bread
75 ml / 3 fl. oz / ⅓ cup extra-virgin olive oil
1 clove of garlic, minced
a small bunch of basil, chopped
salt and freshly ground black pepper
350 g / 12 oz / 2 ⅓ cups vine tomatoes, cored,
    deseeded and chopped

METHOD

- Preheat the grill to a moderately hot temperature.

- Brush both sides of the slices of sourdough with a
  little olive oil, then arrange on a grilling tray. Grill for
  1–2 minutes on each side until lightly charred.

- Stir together the remaining olive oil with the garlic and
  basil. Season the tomatoes, then stir into the oil.

- Spoon the tomatoes onto the sourdough toasts.
  Serve immediately for best results.

Moussaka

Serves: 6   Preparation time: 45 minutes   Cooking time: 20 minutes

INGREDIENTS

2 medium aubergines (eggplants),
    roughly diced
salt and freshly ground black pepper
3 tbsp olive oil
2 small onions, finely chopped
2 cloves of garlic, minced
600 g / 1 lb 5 oz / 4 cups lamb mince
2 tsp dried oregano
1 tsp dried thyme
½ tsp ground cinnamon
200 g / 7 oz / 1 cup canned chopped tomatoes
225 ml / 8 fl. oz / 1 cup lamb stock
75 g / 3 oz / ⅓ cup unsalted butter
75 g / 3 oz / ½ cup plain (all-purpose) flour
750 ml / 1 pint 6 fl. oz / 3 cups whole
    (full-fat) milk
2 small egg yolks
110 g / 4 oz / 1 cup Cheddar, grated
1 large vine tomato, deseeded and
    cut into wedges

METHOD

- Salt the aubergine and arrange on kitchen paper to drain. Pat dry after 10 minutes.
- Heat the oil in a large casserole dish set over a medium heat and sauté the chopped onion and garlic for 4–5 minutes.
- Add the lamb mince and brown all over, then stir in the dried herbs and spices.
- Add the chopped tomatoes and lamb stock and bring to a simmer, then cook for 15 minutes over a reduced heat.
- Preheat the oven to 200°C (180°C fan) / 400F / gas 6.
- Melt the butter in a large saucepan set over a moderate heat, then whisk in the flour to make a roux and cook until golden.
- Whisk in the milk in a slow, steady stream until thickened. Simmer for 5 minutes, then whisk in the egg yolks, cheese and some seasoning.
- Spoon a little of the lamb sauce into the base of a large oval baking dish, then scatter over some aubergine.
- Top with cheese sauce, followed by lamb sauce and then more aubergine around the edges.
- Repeat again, then finish with the fresh tomato on top.
- Bake for 20 minutes until golden brown on top and piping hot in the middle. Leave to stand for 5 minutes before serving.

Lamb Kebabs

Serves: 4   Preparation time: 15 minutes   Cooking time: 6–8 minutes

INGREDIENTS

600 g / 1 lb 5 oz / 4 cups lamb mince
a small bunch of mint leaves, finely chopped
1 red chilli (chili), finely chopped
1 shallot, finely chopped
2 cloves of garlic, minced
1 tsp ground cumin
1 tsp ground coriander
1 tsp paprika
salt and freshly ground black pepper
3 tbsp olive oil

METHOD

- Preheat a grill or barbecue to a moderately hot temperature and soak 8 wooden skewers in cold water.
- Scrunch together the lamb mince with the mint, chilli, shallot, garlic, ground spices and seasoning in a large mixing bowl.
- Shape into 24 small balls, then thread 3 onto each skewer.
- Brush with a little olive oil, then cook under the grill or on the barbecue for 6–8 minutes. Cook until lightly charred and firm to the touch, turning once halfway through.
- Let the kebabs cool slightly before serving.

Ham and Artichoke Pizza

Serves: 4   Preparation time: 15 minutes   Cooking time: 8–10 minutes

INGREDIENTS

250 g / 9 oz ready-made pizza dough
a little plain (all-purpose) flour, for kneading
400 g / 14 oz / 2 cups canned chopped
    tomatoes
150 g / 5 oz / 1 cup buffalo mozzarella balls,
    drained
100 g / 3 ½ oz / ⅔ cup prosciutto slices
200 g / 7 oz / 1 cup canned artichoke hearts,
    drained and sliced
75 g / 3 oz / 1 cup button mushrooms, sliced
3 tbsp sun-dried tomatoes in oil, drained
2 tbsp black olives, pitted
1 tbsp capers, drained
2 tbsp extra-virgin olive oil
salt and freshly ground black pepper
a small handful of rocket (arugula)

METHOD

- Preheat the oven to 220°C (200°C fan) / 425F / gas 7
  and place 2 large circular baking trays in the oven to
  warm up.

- Divide the dough in half and roll out on a floured
  surface into 2 rounds approximately 1 cm (¼ in) thick.

- Remove the trays from the oven and lift the dough onto
  them, then spread with chopped tomatoes.

- Arrange a mixture of the mozzarella, prosciutto,
  artichokes, mushrooms, sun-dried tomatoes, olives
  and capers on top.

- Drizzle with a little oil and season with salt and
  pepper. Bake for 8–10 minutes until the base is golden
  underneath and the mozzarella is melted.

- Remove from the oven and leave to cool slightly, then
  garnish with rocket, season to taste and serve.

Fish and Chips

Serves: 4   Preparation time: 15–20 minutes   Cooking time: 15–20 minutes

INGREDIENTS

1.25 l / 2 pints 4 fl. oz / 5 cups vegetable oil,
    for deep-frying
55 g / 2 oz / ⅓ cup plain (all-purpose) flour
salt and freshly ground black pepper
450 g / 1 lb / 2 cups cod or haddock fillet,
    trimmed and cut into thick strips
2 large eggs, beaten
250 g / 9 oz / 2 cups golden breadcrumbs
500 g / 1 lb 2 oz / 4 cups frozen French fries

METHOD

- Heat the oil in a large, heavy-based saucepan to 180°C / 350F.

- Place the flour in a shallow dish and season with salt and pepper.

- Dust the pieces of fish with the flour, shake off any excess and dip into the beaten egg.

- Once coated, gently roll the fish in the breadcrumbs to coat. Arrange on a lined tray and finish coating all the fish.

- Deep fry the fish in batches for 3–4 minutes until golden brown and crisp.

- Drain the fish on kitchen paper.

- Once all the fish has been fried, keep warm to one side and fry the chips in the hot oil for 3–4 minutes until golden brown all over.

- Drain on kitchen paper before serving with the fish.

Niçoise Salad

Serves: 4   Preparation time: 15 minutes   Cooking time: 2–3 minutes

INGREDIENTS

110 g / 4 oz / 1 cup green (string) beans,
  trimmed
2 green peppers, sliced
2 red peppers, sliced
75 g / 3 oz / ½ cup pitted black olives, sliced
225 g / 8 oz / 1 ¾ cups cooked long grain rice
4 small vine tomatoes, deseeded and diced
400 g / 14 oz / 2 cups canned tuna steak,
  drained
100 ml / 3 ½ fl. oz / ½ cup extra-virgin
  olive oil
a small bunch of flat-leaf parsley,
  finely chopped
salt and freshly ground black pepper
a small handful of basil leaves, to garnish

METHOD

- Cook the green beans in a large saucepan of salted, boiling water for 2–3 minutes until tender, then drain and refresh in iced water.

- Drain well again and toss with the peppers, olives, rice, tomatoes, tuna, olive oil, parsley and seasoning.

- Spoon into a bowl and garnish with basil leaves before serving.

Waffles

Serves: 4   Preparation time: 10–15 minutes   Cooking time: 12–14 minutes

INGREDIENTS

1 tbsp vegetable oil, for greasing
275 g / 10 oz / 1 ¾ cups plain (all-purpose)
   flour, sifted
150 g / 5 oz / ⅔ cup caster (superfine) sugar
2 ½ tsp baking powder
a pinch of salt
2 medium eggs, separated
250 ml / 9 fl. oz / 1 cup whole (full-fat) milk
175 g / 6 oz / ¾ cup unsalted butter, melted
1 tsp vanilla extract
1 tbsp sugar nibs, to garnish

METHOD

- Preheat a waffle iron according to the manufacturer's instructions and grease with vegetable oil.
- Combine the flour, sugar, baking powder and salt in a large mixing bowl and stir briefly.
- Beat the egg yolks in a separate bowl, then add the milk, butter and vanilla extract and beat again briefly. Whisk into the flour mixture until smooth.
- Beat the egg whites in another bowl until stiffly peaked, then fold into the batter.
- Spoon the batter into the preheated waffle iron and cook in batches, according to the manufacturer's instructions, until golden brown.
- Leave to cool briefly on wire racks before garnishing with sugar nibs and serving.

Cherry Clafoutis

Serves: 4   Preparation time: 10–15 minutes   Cooking time: 22–25 minutes

INGREDIENTS

250 ml / 9 fl. oz / 1 cup whole (full-fat) milk
55 ml / 2 fl. oz / ¼ cup double (heavy) cream
110 g / 4 oz / ½ cup caster (superfine) sugar
2 tbsp kirsch (optional)
1 tsp vanilla extract
a pinch of salt
6 large eggs
125 g / 4 ½ oz / ¾ cup plain (all-purpose)
    flour
300 g / 10 ½ oz / 2 cups red cherries
1 tbsp icing (confectioners') sugar

METHOD

• Preheat the oven to 200°C (180°C fan) / 400F / gas 6.

• Combine the milk, cream, sugar, kirsch, vanilla
  extract, salt and eggs in a food processor. Blend
  until combined.

• Add the flour and pulse until a batter comes together.

• Divide the batter between four individual baking dishes
  and stud with cherries.

• Bake for 22–25 minutes until golden on top and
  a skewer comes out clean when inserted into
  their centres.

• Remove from the oven to a wire rack to cool briefly.
  Dust with icing sugar before serving.

Pulled pork
burritos

Fresh ingredients

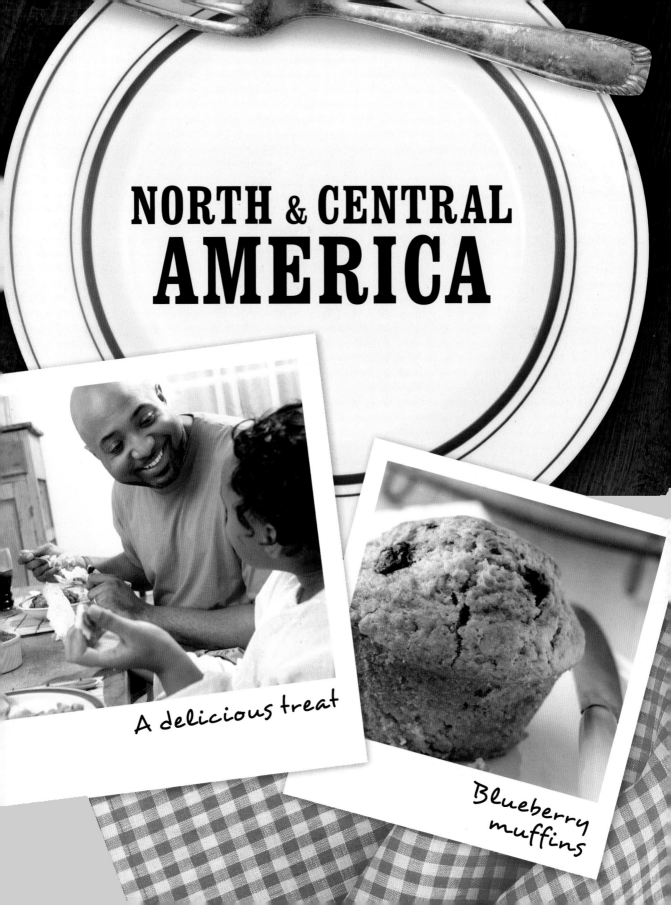

NORTH & CENTRAL AMERICA

A delicious treat

Blueberry
muffins

Huevos Rancheros

Serves: 4   Preparation time: 15 minutes   Cooking time: 15–20 minutes

INGREDIENTS

55 ml / 2 fl. oz / ¼ cup olive oil
1 clove of garlic, minced
1 large onion, finely chopped
1 large red pepper, diced
salt and freshly ground pepper
1 tsp smoked paprika
a pinch of Cayenne pepper
600 g / 1 lb 5 oz / 3 cups canned chopped
   tomatoes
4 medium eggs
a small handful of basil leaves, to garnish

METHOD

- Heat half of the oil in a saucepan set over a medium heat until hot, then add the garlic, onion, pepper and a little salt and sweat for 5–6 minutes until softened.
- Stir in the ground spices and cook for 1 minute, then add the chopped tomatoes.
- Cook steadily for 6–7 minutes, stirring occasionally, until the sauce has thickened slightly, then season to taste.
- Heat the remaining oil in a large frying pan set over a medium heat until hot, then crack in the eggs and fry for 3–4 minutes until set.
- Spoon the tomato and pepper stew into bowls and top with a fried egg, some more seasoning and a few basil leaves before serving.

Pastrami Sandwich

Serves: 4   Preparation time: 5–10 minutes

INGREDIENTS

55 g / 2 oz / ¼ cup plain yoghurt
2 tbsp Dijon mustard
2 tbsp mayonnaise
a squeeze of lemon juice
salt and freshly ground black pepper
8 slices of white sandwich bread
350 g / 12 oz / 2 ⅓ cups pastrami slices
3 large pickles, cut into long slices

METHOD

- Stir together the yoghurt, mustard, mayonnaise, lemon juice and seasoning in a small mixing bowl until smooth.
- Spread half of the slices of bread with the sauce and top with folded slices of pastrami and slices of pickle.
- Position the other slices of bread on top before serving.

Pulled Pork Burrito

Serves: 4   Preparation time: 15–20 minutes   Cooking time: 15–20 minutes

INGREDIENTS

2 tbsp sunflower oil
1 onion, finely chopped
3 cloves of garlic, minced
salt and freshly ground black pepper
1 tsp ground cumin
a pinch of ground cinnamon
a pinch of Cayenne pepper
100 ml / 3 ½ fl. oz / ½ cup tomato ketchup
100 ml / 3 ½ fl. oz / ½ cup cider vinegar
2 tbsp soft dark brown sugar
450 ml / 16 fl. oz / 2 cups chicken stock
800 g / 1 lb 12 oz cooked pork shoulder
75 g / 3 oz / ⅓ cup barbecue sauce
200 g / 7 oz / 1 cup canned chopped tomatoes
a pinch of caster (superfine) sugar
2 tbsp distilled vinegar
1 clove of garlic, minced
a small bunch of coriander (cilantro),
    finely chopped
4 large flour tortillas
100 g / 3 ½ oz / 1 cup Cheddar or
    Monterey Jack, grated
1 avocado, pitted and sliced
2 limes, cut into wedges

METHOD

- Heat the oil in a large casserole dish set over a moderate heat until hot.

- Add the onion and garlic and some seasoning and sweat until golden.

- Add the ground spices, stir well and cook for a further minute, then add the ketchup, vinegar, sugar and chicken stock.

- Bring to a simmer, stirring well, then add the pork. Cook at a gentle simmer for 15–20 minutes until the pork has absorbed some sauce.

- Shred the pork between two forks, then stir in the barbecue sauce and season to taste.

- Mix together the chopped tomatoes, sugar, vinegar, garlic and coriander in a small bowl and season to taste.

- Pile the pulled pork, cheese, avocado and prepared salsa onto the centre of the tortillas, then fold and roll into burritos.

- Serve with lime wedges on the side.

Mac and Cheese

Serves: 4   Preparation time: 20 minutes   Cooking time: 18–20 minutes

INGREDIENTS

350 g / 12 oz / 3 cups macaroni
75 g / 3 oz / ⅓ cup unsalted butter
75 g / 3 oz / ½ cup plain (all-purpose) flour
750 ml / 1 pint 6 fl. oz / 3 cups whole
    (full-fat) milk
2 small egg yolks
225 g / 8 oz / 2 cups Cheddar, grated
salt and freshly ground black pepper
a small handful of basil leaves, to garnish

METHOD

- Preheat the oven to 200°C (180°C fan) / 400F / gas 6.
- Cook the macaroni in a large saucepan of salted, boiling water for 8 minutes, then drain well and refresh in a bowl of tepid water.
- Melt the butter in a large saucepan set over a moderate heat, then whisk in the flour to make a roux and cook until golden.
- Whisk in the milk in a slow, steady stream until thickened. Simmer for 5 minutes, then whisk in the egg yolks, half the cheese and some seasoning.
- Drain the macaroni and add it to the cheese sauce, stirring and folding to coat.
- Divide between four individual gratin dishes, then top with the remaining cheese and bake for 18–20 minutes until golden and bubbling.
- Remove from the oven and leave to stand briefly, then serve with a garnish of basil leaves.

Clam Chowder

Serves: 4   Preparation time: 15 minutes   Cooking time: 25 minutes

INGREDIENTS

3 tbsp unsalted butter
100 g / 3 ½ oz / ⅔ cup pancetta,
    cut into thin lardons
1 small onion, finely chopped
2 sticks of celery, finely sliced
1 clove of garlic, minced
1 large white potato, peeled and finely diced
salt and freshly ground pepper
450 g / 1 lb / 3 cups clams, washed and
    drained
1 l / 1 pint 16 fl. oz / 4 cups vegetable stock
150 ml / 5 fl. oz / ⅔ cup double (heavy)
    cream
a few sprigs of thyme

METHOD

- Melt 1 tbsp of butter in a large saucepan set over a medium heat until hot.

- Add the pancetta lardons and sauté until golden brown and crisp, then remove from the saucepan to a plate lined with kitchen paper.

- Add the remaining butter to the pan and leave to melt, then add the onion, celery, garlic, potato and a little salt.

- Sweat for 8–10 minutes until the potato is softened, then add the clams, stock and three-quarters of the pancetta.

- Bring to a simmer and cover with a lid. Cook for 6–8 minutes until the clams open, discarding any that don't.

- Add the cream and return the soup to a simmer, then season to taste.

- Ladle into bowls and serve with a garnish of thyme and the reserved pancetta.

Caesar Salad

Serves: 4   Preparation time: 10 minutes   Cooking time: 18–22 minutes

INGREDIENTS

2 large skinless chicken breasts
2 tbsp sunflower oil
salt and freshly ground pepper
4 small little gem lettuce
1 tomato, finely sliced
1 small white onion, finely sliced
2 large handfuls of croutons
110 g / 4 oz / ½ cup Caesar dressing
a few sprigs of flat-leaf parsley, to garnish

METHOD

- Heat a griddle pan over a moderate heat until hot, then brush the chicken breasts with sunflower oil and season generously.
- Griddle in the pan for 18–22 minutes, turning occasionally, until lightly charred and cooked through; the chicken should register at least 74°C / 165F on a meat thermometer.
- Let the chicken rest for 5 minutes, then slice into strips.
- Arrange the lettuce on plates and top with the chicken, tomato, onion and croutons before drizzling with dressing.
- Serve immediately with a garnish of flat-leaf parsley.

Crab Cakes

Serves: 4   Preparation time: 25–30 minutes   Cooking time: 9–12 minutes

INGREDIENTS

400 g / 14 oz / 2 ⅔ cups canned crab meat,
    drained
2 spring onions (scallions), finely chopped
a small bunch of coriander (cilantro),
    finely chopped
1 medium egg white, lightly beaten
2 tbsp dark soy sauce
110 ml / 4 fl. oz / ½ cup groundnut or
    sunflower oil
sweet chilli (chili) sauce, to serve

METHOD

- Pick through the crabmeat for any bone and cartilage, then place the crabmeat in a mixing bowl.

- Stir through the spring onions, coriander, egg white and soy sauce and knead gently for 2–3 minutes.

- Shape the mixture into crab cakes and arrange on a lined tray.

- Heat some of the oil in a large frying pan set over a moderate heat until hot and fry the crab cakes in batches for 3–4 minutes, flipping once, until golden brown on both sides.

- Drain the crab cakes on kitchen paper; use a little fresh oil when cooking each batch.

- Serve the cooked crab cakes with pots of sweet chilli sauce on the side for dipping.

Chicken Fajitas

Serves: 4   Preparation time: 15 minutes   Cooking time: 15 minutes

INGREDIENTS

4 chive stalks
3 tbsp sunflower oil
1 large onion, finely sliced
2 cloves of garlic, finely chopped
2 large skinless chicken breasts, sliced
2 tsp ground cumin
1 tbsp smoked paprika
½ tsp chilli (chili) powder
a pinch of caster (superfine) sugar
salt and freshly ground black pepper
2 ripe avocados, pitted and chopped
1 lime, juiced
4 large flour tortillas
1 red pepper, finely diced
75 g / 3 oz / ¾ cup Red Leicester, grated

METHOD

- Blanch the chive stalks in a saucepan of boiling water for 10 seconds, then remove and refresh in iced water.

- Heat the oil in a large sauté pan set over a moderate heat until hot.

- Add the onion and garlic and sauté for 3–4 minutes, then add the chicken.

- Continue to sauté until the chicken is browned all over and cooked through. Sprinkle over the ground spices, sugar and some seasoning, stirring well.

- Cook over a reduced heat for a further minute, then set to one side.

- Mash together the avocado with the lime juice and seasoning until smooth.

- Spread the avocado over the centres of the tortillas, then top with the chicken.

- Top with red pepper and cheese, then fold and tie using the blanched chive stalks.

- Serve immediately.

Flan

Serves: 4   Preparation time: 15–20 minutes   Cooking time: 40–45 minutes

INGREDIENTS

275 g / 10 oz / 1 ¼ cups caster (superfine)
    sugar
55 ml / 2 fl. oz / ¼ cup water
4 medium eggs
1 medium egg yolk
500 ml / 18 fl. oz / 2 cups whole (full-fat)
    milk
2 tsp good-quality vanilla extract
a small handful of mint leaves, to garnish

METHOD

- Preheat the oven to 150°C (130°C fan) / 275°F / gas 1.
- Cook 150 g / 5 oz / ⅔ cup of the sugar with the water in a saucepan set over a moderate heat, swirling the pan occasionally, until a golden caramel forms.
- Pour the caramel into the base of an 18 cm (7 in) round ceramic baking dish and tilt it to coat the surface evenly, then set to one side.
- Whisk together the eggs, egg yolk and remaining sugar in a mixing bowl until smooth, then add the vanilla extract and whisk again briefly before straining into a jug.
- Pour the mixture over the caramel and sit the dish in a roasting tin lined with a damp tea towel.
- Fill the roasting tin with boiling water so that it comes halfway up the side of the baking dish.
- Bake the flan for 40–45 minutes until just set, then remove from the oven and allow it to cool.
- Once cool, carefully invert the flan onto a serving plate and serve with a garnish of mint leaves.

Blueberry Muffins

Makes: 18   Preparation time: 10–15 minutes   Cooking time: 18–22 minutes

INGREDIENTS

non-fat cooking spray, for greasing
450 g / 1 lb / 3 cups plain (all-purpose) flour,
    sifted
225 g / 8 oz / 1 cup caster (superfine) sugar
1 tsp baking powder
½ tsp bicarbonate of (baking) soda
a pinch of salt
75 g / 3 oz / ⅓ cup unsalted butter, melted
    and cooled
125 ml / 4 ½ fl. oz / ½ cup plain yoghurt
2 medium eggs
1 tsp vanilla extract
250 g / 9 oz / 2 cups blueberries

METHOD

- Preheat the oven to 180°C (160°C fan) / 350°F / gas 4 and grease 18 holes of two 12-hole muffin trays with cooking spray.

- Combine the flour, sugar, baking powder, bicarbonate of soda and salt in a large mixing bowl.

- In a separate mixing bowl, whisk together the butter, yoghurt, eggs and vanilla extract until smooth.

- Add to the dry ingredients and fold through until just combined; try not to overmix the batter.

- Gently fold through the blueberries, then divide the batter between 18 holes in the trays.

- Bake for 18–22 minutes until risen, golden and springy to the touch; a toothpick will come out almost clean from the centres when the muffins are ready.

- Remove the trays to a wire rack to cool before turning out the muffins and serving.

Steak with
chimichurri sauce

Date night

SOUTH AMERICA
& THE CARIBBEAN

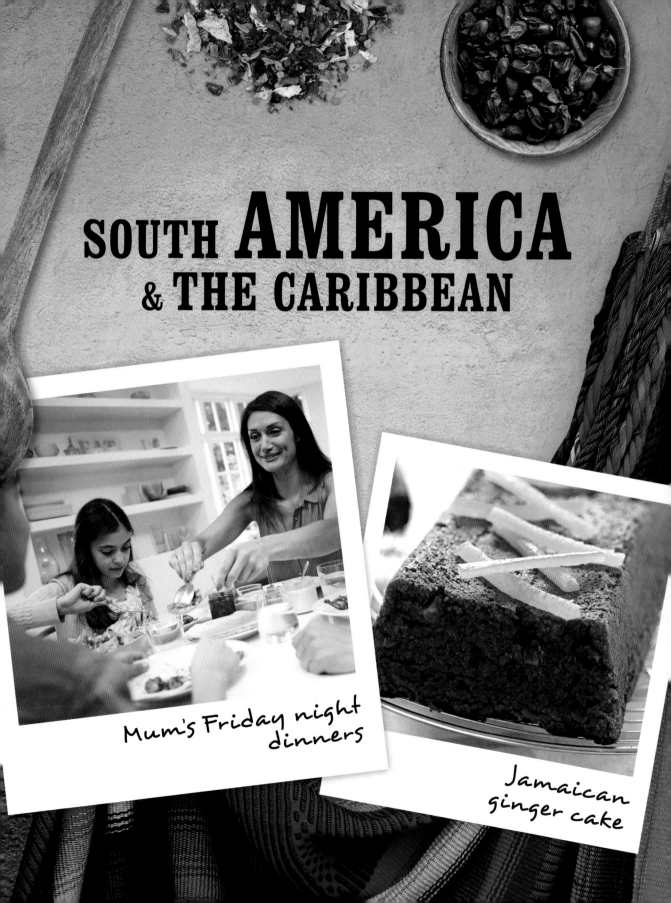

Mum's Friday night dinners

Jamaican ginger cake

Ceviche

Serves: 6   Preparation time: 40 minutes

INGREDIENTS

a small bunch of coriander (cilantro)
300 g / 10 ½ oz / 2 cups skinless cod fillet,
    pin-boned
300 g / 10 ½ oz / 2 cups skinless salmon
    fillet, pin-boned
2 limes, juiced
½ small red chilli (chili), deseeded and
    finely chopped
1 large avocado, stoned and finely diced
1 tsp coriander seeds, crushed
salt and freshly ground black pepper

METHOD

- Cut a few sprigs of coriander from the bunch; finely chop the remaining leaves and place in a mixing bowl.
- Add the fish, lime juice, chilli, avocado, crushed coriander seeds and seasoning.
- Stir well, cover, and chill for 30 minutes.
- Spoon into ramekins and serve chilled.

Steak with Chimichurri Sauce

Serves: 4   Preparation time: 20 minutes   Cooking time: 45–50 minutes

INGREDIENTS

450 g / 1 lb / 3 cups new potatoes
3 tbsp olive oil
flaked sea salt and freshly ground pepper
3 tbsp red wine vinegar
1 shallot, finely chopped
2 red chillies (chilies), deseeded and
    finely chopped
3 cloves of garlic, minced
a small bunch of coriander (cilantro),
    finely chopped
a small handful of oregano, finely chopped
150 ml / 5 fl. oz / ⅔ cup extra-virgin olive oil
2 x 300 g / 10 ½ oz sirloin steaks, trimmed
2 tbsp groundnut oil
1 tbsp unsalted butter, cubed
150 g / 5 oz / 1 ½ cups asparagus spears,
    woody ends removed

METHOD

- Preheat the oven to 200°C (180°C fan) / 400F / gas 6.

- Arrange the potatoes in a roasting tray and drizzle with 1 tbsp of the oil, then season with salt and pepper.

- Roast for 45–50 minutes until tender and crisp on the outsides.

- Prepare the chimichurri by stirring together the red wine vinegar, shallot, chillies, garlic and herbs with the remaining olive oil. Season to taste and set to one side.

- In the meantime, heat a cast-iron frying pan over a high heat until hot. Rub the steaks with groundnut oil and season with salt and pepper.

- Sear in the pan for 3 minutes, then turn and cook for a further minute. Transfer to the oven for 6–8 minutes or until the meat reaches at least 60°C / 140F on a meat thermometer.

- Remove from the oven and leave to rest on a plate, covered loosely with kitchen foil, for 10 minutes.

- Add the asparagus to the pan and dot with butter, then season. Roast in the oven for 4 minutes.

- Remove the asparagus and potatoes when ready.

- Slice the steaks and serve with the asparagus and potatoes and bowls of the chimichurri sauce on the side.

Chicken Accras

Serves: 4   Preparation time: 15 minutes   Cooking time: 8–10 minutes

INGREDIENTS

1.25 l / 2 pints 4 fl. oz / 5 cups vegetable oil,
    plus extra for rolling
a small bunch of coriander (cilantro),
    leaves picked
600 g / 1 lb 5 oz / 4 cups minced chicken
75 g / 3 oz / 1 cup desiccated coconut,
    plus extra to garnish
2 spring onions (scallions), finely sliced
salt and freshly ground black pepper
225 g / 8 oz / 1 ½ cups panko breadcrumbs
2 tbsp salted peanuts, crushed

METHOD

- Heat the oil in a large, heavy-based saucepan to
  180°C / 350F.
- Finely chop three-quarters of the coriander leaves and
  combine with the minced chicken, desiccated coconut,
  spring onions and seasoning in a large mixing bowl.
- Take tablespoons of the mixture and roll into balls
  between oiled palms.
- Roll in breadcrumbs to coat, then deep-fry, in batches,
  for 4–5 minutes until golden brown.
- Drain on kitchen paper, then serve with a garnish
  of desiccated coconut, crushed peanuts and the
  remaining coriander leaves.

Beef Tacos

Serves: 4   Preparation time: 25 minutes   Cooking time: 15–20 minutes

INGREDIENTS

3 tbsp sunflower oil
500 g / 1 lb 2 oz / 3 ⅓ cups lean steak mince
salt and freshly ground black pepper
1 tbsp ground cumin
1 tsp ground coriander
2 tsp smoked paprika
a pinch of caster (superfine) sugar
200 g / 7 oz / 1 cup canned chopped tomatoes
200 g / 7 oz / 1 cup canned red kidney beans,
    drained
125 ml / 4 ½ fl. oz / ½ cup beef stock
2 large ripe avocados, pitted and chopped
½ red onion, finely chopped
1 lime, juiced
a dash of hot sauce
1 red pepper, deseeded and finely diced
1 small cucumber, deseeded and finely diced
½ iceberg lettuce, shredded
½ red onion, finely chopped
a small handful of coriander (cilantro),
    finely chopped
1 lemon, juiced
4 large corn taco shells
100 g / 3 ½ oz / 1 cup Red Leicester,
    finely grated

METHOD

- Heat the sunflower oil in a large casserole dish set over a moderate heat until hot. Add the steak mince and seasoning, browning well all over.

- Add the spices and sugar, then stir well and cook for 1 minute.

- Stir in the chopped tomatoes, kidney beans and beef stock. Bring the mixture to a simmer, then reduce the heat and cook gently for 15–20 minutes.

- Season to taste, then leave to cool slightly to one side.

- Mash together the avocado, red onion, lime juice and hot sauce until smooth, then season to taste and put to one side.

- Mix together the pepper, cucumber, lettuce, red onion and coriander with lemon juice and seasoning in a mixing bowl.

- Spoon the beef into the taco shells, then top with the chopped salad.

- Serve with the cheese and guacamole on the side.

Spicy Fish Stew

Serves: 4   Preparation time: 15 minutes   Cooking time: 20 minutes

INGREDIENTS

2 tbsp olive oil
2 cloves of garlic, minced
1 small red chilli (chili), deseeded and
   finely diced
225 g / 8 oz / 1 ⅓ cups giant couscous
225 g / 8 oz / 1 ½ cups baby plum tomatoes
750 ml / 1 pint 6 fl. oz / 3 cups fish stock
225 g / 8 oz / 1 cup passata
300 g / 10 ½ oz / 2 cups clams,
   washed and drained
225 g / 8 oz / 1 ½ cups squid rings
350 g / 12 oz piece of tuna steak
1 tbsp groundnut oil
salt and freshly ground black pepper
a small handful of mint leaves

METHOD

• Heat the olive oil in a casserole dish set over a medium heat until hot, then add the garlic, chilli and couscous.

• Cook for 4–5 minutes, stirring occasionally, then add the plum tomatoes.

• Cover with the fish stock and passata. Bring to a simmer, then add the clams and squid rings.

• Cover and cook over a reduced heat for 8–10 minutes until the clams have opened and the squid is tender; discard any clams that don't open.

• Meanwhile, heat a frying pan over a moderate heat until hot. Brush the tuna steak with groundnut oil and season with salt and pepper.

• Sear the tuna for 1 minute on each side until golden, then remove from the pan and leave to rest briefly before cutting into chunks and adding to the stew.

• Season the stew to taste, then ladle into bowls and serve with a garnish of mint leaves.

Jerk Chicken

Serves: 4   Preparation time: 20 minutes   Cooking time: 25–30 minutes

INGREDIENTS

4 small chicken breasts, trimmed
3 tbsp sunflower oil
2 tbsp jerk spice mix
½ small butternut squash, peeled and cubed
250 g / 9 oz / 1 ½ cups basmati rice,
    rinsed thoroughly and drained
400 g / 14 oz / 2 cups canned black beans,
    drained
675 ml / 1 pint 4 fl. oz / 2 ¾ cups chicken
    stock
1 lime, cut into wedges
salt and freshly ground black pepper

METHOD

- Preheat the oven to 190°C (170°C fan) / 375F / gas 5 and line a baking tray with aluminium foil.

- Rub the chicken breasts with 2 tbsp of oil, then sprinkle with the jerk spice mix and arrange on the baking tray.

- Bake for 25–30 minutes until firm to the touch.

- Meanwhile, heat the remaining oil in a large saucepan set over a medium heat until hot.

- Add the squash and sauté for 2–3 minutes, then add the rice. Continue to cook for 2 minutes, stirring occasionally, then stir in the beans and stock.

- Bring to the boil, then cover with a lid and cook over a reduced heat for 15–20 minutes until the rice and beans are tender.

- Once the rice has absorbed the stock, remove it from the heat and keep covered for 5–10 minutes, then fluff with a fork and season to taste.

- Remove the chicken once cooked and leave to rest for 5 minutes.

- Spoon the rice into bowls and top with the chicken, then serve with a garnish of lime wedges.

Jamaican Ginger Cake

Serves: 8   Preparation time: 15 minutes   Cooking time: 1 hour 15–25 minutes

INGREDIENTS

175 g / 6 oz / 1 ¼ cups plain (all-purpose)
    flour
1 tsp ground ginger
½ tsp ground cinnamon
a pinch of salt
150 g / 5 oz / ½ cup golden syrup
75 ml / 3 fl. oz / ⅓ cup warm water
85 g / 3 ½ oz / ½ cup dark brown soft sugar
75 g / 3 oz / ⅓ cup unsalted butter, softened
2 cm / 1 in piece of fresh ginger,
    peeled and grated
1 large egg, beaten
2 tbsp whole (full-fat) milk
½ tsp bicarbonate of (baking) soda
candied orange peel, to garnish

METHOD

- Preheat the oven to 170°C (150°C fan) / 325F / gas
  3 and grease and line a 900 g (2 lb) loaf tin with
  greaseproof paper.
- Sift the flour, ground spices and salt into a large
  mixing bowl, then set to one side.
- Combine the golden syrup, water, sugar, butter and
  fresh ginger in a large saucepan.
- Cook over a medium heat until syrupy, then beat
  the syrup into the flour mixture until you have a
  smooth batter.
- Beat in the egg in stages, then beat in the milk and
  bicarbonate of soda.
- Scrape the batter into the prepared loaf tin and bake
  for 1 hour 15–25 minutes until risen. Test with a
  wooden toothpick; if it comes out clean, the cake
  is done.
- Remove to a wire rack to cool. Once cool, turn out from
  the tin and serve with candied orange peel on top.

Coconut Manjar

Serves: 4   Preparation time: 2 hours 15 minutes   Cooking time: 20 minutes

INGREDIENTS

1 l / 1 pint 16 fl. oz / 4 cups whole (full-fat) milk
250 ml / 9 fl. oz / 1 cup coconut milk
1 tbsp cornflour (cornstarch)
1 tsp vanilla extract
1 tbsp vegetable oil, for greasing
white chocolate biscuit sticks
1 tsp liquid glucose, warmed
2 tbsp silver dragee balls, to garnish
55 g / 2 oz / ⅔ cup desiccated coconut

METHOD

- Combine the milk, coconut milk, cornflour and vanilla extract in a saucepan.
- Whisk until the cornflour dissolves, then cook over a medium heat and bring to a simmer.
- Cook at a simmer, stirring frequently, for 12–15 minutes until thickened into a thick custard.
- Grease four individual dessert moulds with vegetable oil. Divide the custard between the moulds and leave to cool for 15 minutes.
- Cover the moulds and chill for 2 hours or until set.
- Brush the biscuit sticks with liquid glucose, then roll half in the dragee balls and half in the desiccated coconut.
- Unmould the manjar onto serving plates. Serve with a garnish of remaining desiccated coconut and dragee balls as well as the biscuit sticks.

Index

Picture Credits

4–5 Lew Robertson / Getty Images, 9 (tr) DEA Picture Library / Getty Images
3, 6, 7, 8-9, 30–31, 62–63, 86–87, 108–109 © Thinkstock / Getty Images
Food photography and recipe development: PhotoCuisine UK and StockFood